The Queens represent intuition and receptive energy and the strength we all have coming from those places.

REMEMBER TO BREATHE

TRUST YOUR FEELINGS

KEEP GOING

MANY Queens TAROT

All art and words by
LETTIE JANE RENNEKAMP

Andrews McMeel
PUBLISHING®

SIMPLE SPREADS FOR TAROT CARDS:

◊ Draw one card daily, what is your lesson here?

◊ Ask the deck a question and draw a card in response.

◊ Draw one card for your moon side and one card for your sun side.

◊ Draw three cards for past / present / future.

◊ Draw three cards for who you are today / what you need to know about it / where you are going.

◊ Draw three cards for your head / your heart / your path.

◊ Take time at the new moon / full moon / during hard times, pull as many cards as you need to define a life path for yourself.

If something doesn't resonate, pull another card or use another resource to look up alternative interpretations. I've written these short descriptions for each card based on my own (totally biased and limited) tarot knowledge, please infuse these cards with your own interpretations as needed.

Ask a friend or several friends to help you interpret the cards you draw. Collective wisdom and discussion can always help unlock meaning. Bring your tarot cards with you when you travel or go out.

Thank you to everyone who has supported or helped this tarot deck, especially Michael Buchino, Amy Subach, Guy Martelet, Anne Parmeter, Kacey Meyer, Amelia Pillow, Erin Aquarian, Billy Rennekamp, and Ira Leigh.

MAJOR ARCANA

0 THE FOOL: The time to start is now. Big hopes, blind luck. **REVERSED:** Prepare yourself to start. Pack your bags, check your water supply.

1 THE MAGICIAN: Magic is energy with purpose, believe in your own power, call on your allies, and make it happen. **REVERSED:** If you feel disillusioned, clarify your intentions with yourself. Tap into your own self-worth and know that you are entitled to your own power.

2 THE HIGH PRIESTESS: You know the darkness, you know the light, behind your eyelids is your eyesight. Let the priestess in and feel more aware of living, loving, and being. **REVERSED:** You may feel out of sync with your intuition or your guides, spend quiet time remembering what you really want.

3 THE EMPRESS: Luscious softness is in your air tonight, dance with your earthly riches and let yourself be. **REVERSED:** Are you withholding from your garden or the earth? Remember the ebb and flow of natural energy.

4 THE EMPEROR: You can build what you need from the resources at hand. You are capable and in charge. **REVERSED:** It's okay to feel let down, make peace here and come back when you are ready to work things out diplomatically.

5 THE HIEROPHANT: What benefit do you find in conforming to the collective? Which history was written to hold you inside it? Put your voice inside the system to be heard. **REVERSED:** Breaking free of the system, coloring outside the lines, leaving the church behind.

6 THE LOVERS: To connect, to love in the endless cycle of loving, fucking, and tumbling into each other and back out again. This is where our souls merge. **REVERSED:** There is some disconnect, some discontent. It's not all there, if it was once or never has been. Reach outside the bubble you have made.

7 THE CHARIOT: Driving horses of darkness and light doesn't guarantee success, but it's a pretty good omen. Willpower is the key. **REVERSED:** All your plans feel like they are falling apart. Go back to the last place you felt secure and work from there.

8 STRENGTH: You have grit. Tame the lion inside you with gentleness; when hard times come, know that you are enough. **REVERSED:** Your courage is failing you. Treat what feels like weakness with gentleness and ask your community to help you move through tough times.

9 THE HERMIT: Take all the time you need to look inside. **REVERSED:** Perhaps you have been spending too much time with other people, or you are feeling isolated. Remember to be a good partner to yourself.

10 THE WHEEL OF FORTUNE: Events are changing outside of your control; the wheel of life turns and you can adapt to change, as you have before and will again.

REVERSED: Are you struggling against external changes? Ask yourself why, and challenge yourself to adapt.

11 JUSTICE: You are acting in balance. Remember that judging others is only another form of self-reflection. You have the knowledge to act with integrity. **REVERSED:** Acknowledge where you may have made mistakes; seek balance to feel at peace again.

12 THE HANGED MAN: Take no action and find peace in discomfort. The answer is found after relinquishing control. **REVERSED:** Stop struggling to find the answer, it will come to you once you relax.

13 DEATH: The garden must die back in the winter to be reborn in the spring. The snake sheds its skin and makes room for new growth. **REVERSED:** Are you trying to keep something from dying? Make peace with letting go and sitting fallow so new growth can come forth next season.

14 TEMPERANCE: Just dip your toe in to see how it feels. Mixing elements from all areas of your life puts you in peace and balance. **REVERSED:** Have you been making rash decisions? Over-indulging or going to extremes? Let these habits die back and find balance in harmonizing different pieces of your life together.

15 THE DEVIL: What are you chained to? Your addictions may be ideas, habits, sex, or substance, try to remember who is in charge of who. Find healthy sources of pleasure. **REVERSED:** You are coming unbound. Addictions you may have suffered from are still present, but the reins of your life are your own again.

16 THE TOWER: Cataclysmic destruction makes way for radical growth. Brace yourself for change and soften around it. **REVERSED:** You can't stay inside a crumbling structure. Free yourself from expectations and embrace change.

17 THE STAR: There is hope and peace, and it is strong. **REVERSED:** Are you feeling insecure or helpless? Remember on the other side of great change there is hope.

18 THE MOON: Look for the reflected light in the darkness. Don't be afraid of your shadow. It's safe here with us. **REVERSED:** Avoiding your shadow self will only delay growth. Be brave and try to find comfort in dark emotions.

19 THE SUN: The sun illuminates all the light around you, radiance doesn't need to be contained. **REVERSED:** There aren't enough clouds during daylight to cause total darkness, the sun always pulls through.

20 JUDGMENT: The call to decide has come, you can answer it, just look under your wings and make decisions with your heart. **REVERSED:** You are avoiding a call to action. Know that you have the strength to answer, and use your inner eye to make the decision.

21 THE WORLD: The cycle is complete. Pat yourself on the back for whatever you have accomplished, it looks good. **REVERSED:** Perhaps you are one piece away from completing the project, perhaps you are starting over. The good news is, it's the whole world you are working with.

CUPS

ACE: Love, emotional insight, and feeling rush forth, enjoy this gushing experience and act from the heart. **REVERSED:** Are you avoiding your emotional landscape? It is rich with love and intuition, it's okay to tap into that waterfall.

2: Lovers or friends feeling awash in their reciprocal energy. Two snakes almost ready to intertwine. Feeling understood. **REVERSED:** Feeling blocked or isolated from another individual. Remember to love and partner to yourself first, reach out from that place.

3: We built this place on love and friendship. You are held. **REVERSED:** Feeling isolated or alone in a group? Reach out to an individual to feel understood again.

4: Are you unaware of the 4th cup being offered to you? Do you feel bored or disillusioned by what you have? Open yourself to new ideas or possibilities. **REVERSED:** It's okay to take some time to sit under the tree, think about what motivates you, and begin to unravel your mild melancholy.

5: Loss is here and you have the capacity to feel it. It will not last forever. **REVERSED:** You are ready to move on from that deep hurt, start picking up the pieces of your life, baby steps.

6: It's playtime, nostalgia is perfect, just be aware when you are drinking its sweet nectar. **REVERSED:** (This card has a horizontal orientation, therefore it incorporates upright and reversed meanings simultaneously.)

7: You are rich in fantasies and ideas, but don't let them drive you to distraction; rather, be inspired and take action from there. **REVERSED:** All your ideas are pouring out around you; you may feel lost and confused. Take small steps, make a list, ground yourself.

8: Walk away, ride a horse away. Endings aren't always easy, but the past passes away and the sun keeps rising and falling in the sky. **REVERSED:** You might be refusing to leave a situation or staying past your welcome. Ask a friend (or a horse) for help to walk away.

9: Life is gentle, enjoy your pleasures, great and small. There is sunshine on your stretch pants. **REVERSED:** Are you forgetting to be grateful for what you have? Practice enjoying simple pleasures.

10: Your chosen family is here for you. Let yourself be held. **REVERSED:** Are you feeling a little out of place in your family or community? You get to decide who is important to you and be vulnerable where you feel safe.

THE PAGE: Inspiration strikes, take talking to your guides (little fishes, etc.) seriously. You are the student, being distracted can be part of the process. **REVERSED:** Are you lost in the details? Do you feel like a student without a teacher? Look, listen, and learn; be okay with being inspired.

THE KNIGHT: You may be wearing your heart on your sleeve and charming the devil out of the earth. Daydreams come to light and tears come as easy as romance. There's precious cargo here, be gentle now. **REVERSED:** You may be running too far ahead with your heart and your dreams and schemes; beware the unreality of an ungrounded romance.

THE QUEEN: You have all the answers you need, here in the space between your heart and your feet. Act from the guts, the pelvic floor; your divine intuition knows when to laugh and when to cry. **REVERSED:** Are you blocking your ability to feel something fully? Stop telling yourself a story, breathe inside, and find out what's really going on.

THE KING: Don't be afraid of all your softness; you have the power to feel through this situation. **REVERSED:** When your emotions rule everything around you, no one wins.

PENTACLES

ACE: This is a golden moment, seize the opportunity, go forth. Your riches are earthly, your work is strong, and you are full of potential. **REVERSED:** Are you seized by scarcity? Bring your bank accounts up to date and remember small details that make you feel rich, even when money feels scarce.

2: You are balancing so many acts in life, are you bleeding or laughing? **REVERSED:** If you feel like you are dropping the ball, it's okay—you can pick it back up again when you're ready.

3: You can make your plans come to fruition with the help of a few key people. **REVERSED:** You may be feeling out of sync with a project or your team, reconnect with the individuals to make the group feel whole again.

4: Boundaries are blessings, but are you holding on to keep others out? Is your relationship to wealth or security allowing for love and abundance? **REVERSED:** You may be letting material wealth pass through you; you are not in control here. Reassess how you measure wealth.

5: Have you been beat down by expectations of abundance and wealth? This is just part of the cycle; there is wealth after destitution. **REVERSED:** Perhaps things are not so bad as they might seem. Look around for the resources you have, you have not hit rock bottom.

6: Who has power over who here? Are you feeling held or held hostage? Ask yourself where you need to give to break free. **REVERSED:** Your sense of your own power is getting out of hand, check yourself.

7: Assess what you've accomplished, it's real nice. Decide to go from here. **REVERSED:** Slow down, don't cut corners, take the time to look at what you're doing.

8: Making progress, slowly, methodically completing the task at hand. **REVERSED:** Are you trying to rush ahead to complete something? Take a deep breath and pay attention to the task at hand.

9: You've achieved a level of luxury through hard work and self-reliance. Reflect on how far you've come and how you got there. **REVERSED:** There's a lack of responsibility or self-reliance; it's time to tow the line.

10: The community that braids together, stays together— sisters, mothers, friends, children, lovers, helpers, humans. **REVERSED:** You may be feeling disconnected or adrift without family or community.

THE PAGE: You are strong. Your foundation is being built, don't wrestle against yourself, and try not to rush growth. **REVERSED:** You may be feeling distracted or disinterested. Rest, and come back to the task when you are refreshed.

THE KNIGHT: Don't get too lost in your own reflection, work is important, but don't leave play behind. **REVERSED:** Remember that magic is in the earth below you. You might be feeling lethargic, so connect with the earth to be refreshed.

THE QUEEN: Feeling deeply, physically satisfied. Your creature comforts are taken care of. **REVERSED:** You may be feeling ungrounded or your intuition is off. Turn to the earth to reconnect, enjoy simple physical pleasures.

THE KING: Solid like a bull, think it through, act from the point of deeply grounded abundance. **REVERSED:** You may be feeling unstable. Remember to play in the dirt, don't take yourself so seriously, and pay attention to detail.

Swords

ACE: Where your thoughts start, your mind will follow. Proceed with your truth. **REVERSED:** If you are having trouble communicating, shut your mouth and listen.

2: Meditate on the mantra: healthy boundaries. Who do you want to keep out and who comes in? **REVERSED:** It's time to let your boundaries down, letting vulnerability in.

3: Heartbreak pierces the heart like a knife, but the sooner you face it, the sooner you can see what opens up around it. **REVERSED:** The heartbreak you thought was coming isn't as bad as you feared.

4: Take a pause, it won't feel like death, it'll feel like life. **REVERSED:** It's time to wake up, playing dead won't help you now.

5: Perhaps you won the conflict, but at what cost? What really pushes others away? **REVERSED:** Perhaps you are feeling the despair left after a conflict. Walk away or go back and take a rest; let the feelings tell you where to go.

6: There are burdens and there is hope; your progress is in continuing. Shoot for the moon and count your steps. **REVERSED:** Rest at the bottom of the staircase and make sure the direction you sought was your own.

7: What are you really getting away with here? Is isolation working for you? **REVERSED:** If you've been caught being dishonest with yourself or others, apologize, ask for forgiveness (grant it to yourself), and learn from your mistakes.

8: Are you bound in self-imposed isolation? Perhaps your thoughts are keeping you from seeing the situation clearly. Breathe. **REVERSED:** The situation is becoming clearer, your ideas make more sense, you can start to move your body again.

9: So many swords cut to the heart of your nightmares. Remember you are both the witness and the author of your thoughts; be gentle. **REVERSED:** You may be feeling oppression, don't hurt yourself. This too will pass.

10: Things can't get much worse. The sun is hiding just over the hill, when you reach rock bottom the only way to go is up. **REVERSED:** The swords are falling out of your back. Perhaps the situation is not as bleak as you thought it might be.

THE PAGE: Excitement about ideas, talking, writing, poetry, and intellectual pursuits resonate with you right now. **REVERSED:** You may be feeling a little foggy, get some good rest, eat well, drink water, and process your ideas.

THE KNIGHT: Your ideas leap ahead, your words rush forth, be reasonable and careful not to cut those around you. **REVERSED:** (This card has a horizontal orientation, therefore it incorporates upright and reversed meanings simultaneously.)

THE QUEEN: Queens can use language like a knife that cleans the wound or creates it, you've got a way with words, speak your truth. **REVERSED:** Remember the words you use on yourself directly manifest your feelings. Connect with your heart to speak honestly.

THE KING: You are able to organize and excite with your ideas and your words. Trust in your vision; the coyote has your back. **REVERSED:** If you are feeling confused about what to say, think about the outcome you would like to achieve and speak to that.

WANDS

ACE: Light a match and run with the sparklers; the time to start is now and your energy is abundant. **REVERSED:** Has something dampened your fire? Tend to practical matters to rekindle the flame.

2: Big, big plans, you are likely to be successful, just keep in touch with what you really want. **REVERSED:** Your plans just can't connect. Warm up your feet and remember the excitement you started with.

3: Looking to the future, take the long view and make a plan. You've got this. **REVERSED:** You may be obsessed by the grand plan and neglecting to think things through or plan wisely.

4: It looks like you are about to be satisfied with where you're hanging out. Stable fire, luscious growth.
REVERSED: Are you feeling a little let down or lonely? Rekindle your inspiration by going over what excited you in the first place.

5: Do you get off on conflict? Is that benefiting you?
REVERSED: Have you been spending all your time untangling other people's messes? Go home and rest.

6: Herald your accomplishments, you've done this and you should be proud. Great art is not made for closets.
REVERSED: It's time to reflect on what you've accomplished and sing the ballad of it to your friends.

7: Your defiance is your strength. Continue fighting the good fight and believe in yourself. **REVERSED:** Stop fighting and let yourself rest.

8: So many wands in the air, you are sure to hit something, act on what you've been thinking about. **REVERSED:** Are you overwhelmed or distracted by everything you hear? Sit down and take a break.

9: You've been through the ringer, but you are still standing and the sun is coming up. **REVERSED:** Ready yourself to make amends and forget old grievances, now is not the time to fight.

10: Are you trying to do too much? Other approaches are possible, you can ask for help. Don't defend the need to be perfect. **REVERSED:** You have been letting go of some of your burdens, do you feel lighter?

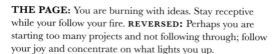

THE PAGE: You are burning with ideas. Stay receptive while your follow your fire. **REVERSED:** Perhaps you are starting too many projects and not following through; follow your joy and concentrate on what lights you up.

THE KNIGHT: Your excitement and confidence is contagious: travel, explore, follow your own lead. **REVERSED:** Sometimes the failure of big plans or ideas seems like a reflection on who you are. Reflect on what you've learned instead.

THE QUEEN: The queen loves life. She is passionate, carnal, and deeply rooted in herself, feel that. **REVERSED:** Have you not been acknowledging your passions? You run the risk of obscuring your motivations if you hide from yourself for too long.

THE KING: Great lizard in life, there is heat in your body and your soul, creative energy is yours, but don't be blinded by your own force. **REVERSED:** Has your passion been dampened? There are times when the fire burns too brightly; decide how much energy you have to give and where.

For years I read the tarot with the tiny booklet inserted in my
Aquarius Tarot deck and discussed the potential meanings
with my friends. I got so much out of those conversations and
I believe trusting your gut and your friends is a great way to
read tarot.

As my obsession with tarot grew, I drew on other resources
and influences, such as:

Seventy-Eight Degrees of Wisdom: A Book of Tarot
by Rachel Pollack

The Way of Tarot: The Spiritual Teacher in the Cards
by Alejandro Jodorowsky and Marianne Costa

The guidebook to The Slow Holler Tarot was very
influential to me. It felt like a healing resource rather than
a lecture. So many of their interpretations gave advice instead
of feedback and I loved the way that made me feel empow-
ered even after a melancholy reading.

Sometimes I search the internet for card interpretations. I've
never picked a particular website that I find affinity with; I
generally scramble through a few pages until I find
a line or paragraph that seems to make everything clear.

I love the Strange Magic podcast with Sarah Faith
Gottesdiener and Amanda Yates Garcia.

Enjoy your tarot journey and thank you for buying
this deck,

Lettie Jane

- ◊ This tarot deck was created to help define a more inclusive definition of femininity, beauty, and body image.

- ◊ This deck is for anyone else who likes to look at tarot cards, and laugh, and feel that there is space for their version of beauty.

- ◊ The characters in this deck are here to blend the boundaries between gender, love, identity, family, friendship, shape, and size.

- ◊ May we love the beauty in our differences and explore the love we can find in ourselves.

www.lettiejane.com @lettiejanemakes